D1289005

OUR MISSION - Henry Ford Museum & Greenfield Village provides unique educational experiences based on authentic objects, stories, and lives from America's traditions of ingenuity, resourcefulness, and innovation. Our purpose is to inspire people to learn from these traditions to help shape a better future.

HENRY FORD MUSEUM

Henry Ford could have afforded to purchase great works of art by the truckload, but instead, he chose to collect commonplace items like toasters, farm machinery, kerosene lamps, steam engines, and several historic buildings. Ford began storing these items on property next to his engineering laboratory while his 12-acre museum building and 81-acre outdoor village site were being constructed.

On September 27, 1928, Thomas Edison pushed a small garden spade once owned by botanist Luther Burbank into a block of hardening concrete that would eventually become the cornerstone for Ford's new museum. One year later, on October 21, 1929, over 100 dignitaries, including President Herbert Hoover and Thomas Edison himself, attended formal dedication ceremonies inside the partially completed building.

The dedication date was selected to commemorate the fiftieth anniversary of Thomas Edison's invention of the first practical incandescent lamp and electric lighting system. The museum was originally named The Edison Institute in honor of Ford's mentor and friend, Thomas A. Edison. After Ford's death in 1947, it was renamed Henry Ford Museum, although The Edison Institute remained as the registered legal name for the whole complex.

▼ **MUSEUM CORNERSTONE** - Thomas Edison signs his name in wet concrete as Henry Ford looks on —September 27, 1928. Ford believed the cornerstone symbolized the union between agriculture and industry in mankind's technological progress.

◄ Thomas Edison's footprints and signature, as well as Luther Burbank's garden spade, can still be seen in the cornerstone which stands in the main entrance hallway of Henry Ford Museum.

▲ Henry Ford Museum was built specifically to be a museum. Henry Ford insisted that all of the public areas of the museum were to be located on one floor. The main exhibition hall—with its distinctive teak flooring—is a single 8-acre room!

▲ The front facade of Henry Ford Museum includes a full-sized replica of Philadelphia's Independence Hall. By duplicating this historic structure, Ford incorporated one of the best-known symbols of American freedom into a building designed to celebrate the accomplishments of American innovators.

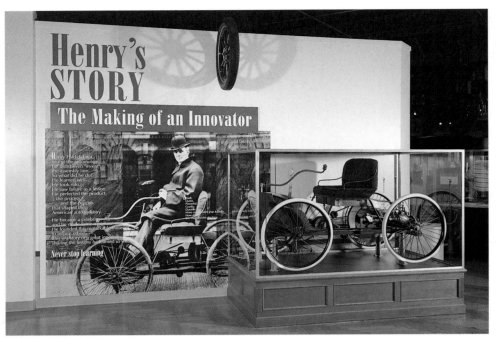

▲ HENRY FORD'S FIRST CAR - Henry Ford built his first car, which he called the "Quadricycle," in a shed behind the house he was renting in Detroit. He drove his Quadricycle for the first time in June 1896. The story of Henry Ford's life from farm boy to industrialist is explored in the exhibition, *Henry's Story: The Making of an Innovator*. Ford's original Quadricycle is one of the featured artifacts.

▲ The Model T was the car that made Henry Ford famous. Over 15 million were produced between 1908-1927, making it one of the most successful automobiles in history. In *Henry's Story: The Making of an Innovator*, visitors can sit behind the wheel of this 1917 Ford Model T.

4

⋀ *OLD 16 - AN AMERICAN RACING LEGEND* - This 1906 Locomobile race car, known as "Old 16," was the first American car to win the Vanderbilt Cup, an international race involving some of the world's best cars and drivers. By winning the race in 1908, "Old 16" proved that American race cars could beat the best that Europe had to offer. "Old 16" is the centerpiece of the museum's newest multimedia exhibit experience.

⋀ Driver George Robertson and mechanic Glenn Ethridge are shown rounding a corner during the 1908 Vanderbilt Cup race on Long Island, New York. Brown Brothers, Sterling, PA.

▲ THE *AUTOMOBILE IN AMERICAN LIFE* -
America's premier exhibition of automotive history
explores the impact the car has made on life in the
United States during the twentieth century. Over 100
vintage automobiles and hundreds of related objects
are displayed in this 60,000 square foot exhibition,
including one of the earliest horseless carriages and
several concept cars.

▲ This rare, hand-carved Lalique crystal hood
ornament is typical of the kind of detail that
was found on luxury cars of the 1920s.

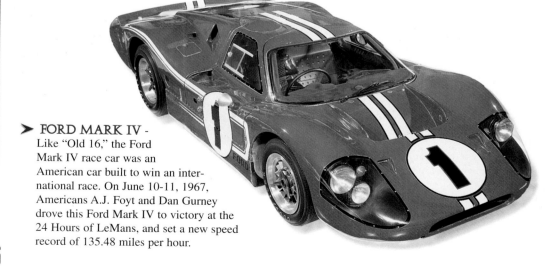

➤ FORD MARK IV -
Like "Old 16," the Ford
Mark IV race car was an
American car built to win an international race. On June 10-11, 1967,
Americans A.J. Foyt and Dan Gurney
drove this Ford Mark IV to victory at the
24 Hours of LeMans, and set a new speed
record of 135.48 miles per hour.

▼ **WIENERMOBILE** - The Oscar Mayer Wienermobile is one of the world's most famous *productmobiles* - a vehicle that looks like the product it is advertising. Wienermobiles like this one, built in 1952, traveled all across the United States to promote Oscar Mayer products.

➤ The *Automobile in American Life* exhibition shows how rapidly the car changed America in the twentieth century. In the 1940s, small restaurants like Lamy's Diner, originally from Marlboro, Massachusetts, provided motorists with a bright and convenient place to get a snack or a warm meal. A few years later, nationwide fast-food franchises would capture the bulk of the motoring public's business. This McDonald's sign was originally erected in 1960 at a McDonald's restaurant located in Madison Heights, Michigan.

▲ Today Lamy's Diner does not serve food, but has been restored to look as it did when Clovis Lamy opened it for business in 1946.

➤ ORIENT "ORITEN" - Before automobiles, bicycle companies created special vehicles to help advertise their products. In 1896, the 23-foot-long, 305-pound Orient Oriten was featured at local bicycle meets to help promote the Orient line of bicycles. The Oriten could reach speeds of 45 miles per hour, but it was extremely difficult to ride, and like most bikes during the 1890s, had no brakes.

◄ CONCORD COACH - Not all of the vehicles on display are motorized. Stagecoaches, like this example built in Concord, New Hampshire in 1865, were pulled by teams of four to six horses and carried passengers in the days before rail service and the automobile.

➤ HARLEY-DAVIDSON MOTORCYCLE - Built in 1941, this classic motorcycle featured a "knucklehead engine," so-named because of the shape of the engine block. An extra passenger or luggage could be carried in the side car.

▲ ALLEGHENY LOCOMOTIVE - Stretching 125-feet long and weighing over 600 tons, the Allegheny was one of the most powerful steam locomotives ever manufactured. Built in Lima, Ohio in 1941, the Allegheny was designed to haul coal from West Virginia over the Allegheny mountains to factories in the North. The Allegheny could pull 160 coal cars, each with a 60-ton load, but was almost immediately challenged by smaller, more powerful diesel locomotives that were also less expensive to operate. The fleet of Allegheny locomotives was retired by 1956 and all but two were scrapped. Today, Allegheny #1601 is the single most photographed object in the museum!

▲ INNOVATION STATION -The only one of its kind anywhere, this giant human-powered learning game introduces fun challenges to players who test their problem-solving skills by directing brightly colored balls through a system of interconnecting tubes.

◄ FLIVVER PLANE - The museum's wide aisles and vaulted ceilings allow for the display of many large artifacts, such as the 1926 Ford "Flivver" plane. Henry Ford originally envisioned this aircraft as an affordable and reliable "Model T of the Air." Three of these experimental planes were built. However, Ford abandoned the project after one of the Flivver planes crashed, killing the test pilot.

▲ PRESIDENTIAL PARADE VEHICLES - One of the museum's most intriguing exhibitions is the display of parade vehicles used by American presidents. The Kennedy Presidential Car is probably the most famous. President John F. Kennedy was riding in this car when he was shot in Dallas in 1963. This modified 1961 Lincoln Continental convertible originally had no armor or bullet-proof glass – its purpose was to provide the President with comfortable transportation and high visibility. After the assassination, the car was basically rebuilt. Titanium armor and bullet-proof glass was installed and later a permanent hard top was added. The car returned to government service and was used by Presidents Johnson, Nixon, Ford and Carter before being retired in 1977. Parade vehicles used by Presidents Theodore Roosevelt, Franklin Roosevelt, Truman, Eisenhower, Reagan and Bush are on display.

◄ LINCOLN CHAIR - President Abraham Lincoln was sitting in this rocking chair in a theater in Washington, D.C. when he was assassinated in 1865. Henry Ford admired Lincoln and acquired this chair from descendants of the original owners.

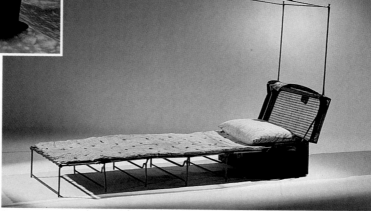

➤ WASHINGTON'S CAMP BED - George Washington actually slept on this folding camp bed when he commanded the Continental Army during the American Revolutionary War in the 1770s. This camp bed was a very handy gadget, folding up into a trunk when not in use.

MADE IN AMERICA

▲ *MADE IN AMERICA* - Featuring robots, overhead conveyors, steam engines and other mechanical devices, the 50,000 square-foot exhibition explores how the production of goods impacts our society.

▼ TRIPLE EXPANSION ENGINE GENERATOR - Weighing 190 tons, this engine was developed by Thomas Edison and installed in 1891 in a central electrical power station in New York City. The three vertical steam engines in the center produce 635 horsepower to drive the 200 kilowatt direct current (DC) generators at each end of the machine.

A wide assortment of engines can be found in the *Made in America* exhibition, from the world's oldest surviving steam engine (built in 1760) to the ceremonial switch that started the world's first commercial nuclear power plant.

▲ TOWER OF POWER - How much muscle power does it take to energize a series of light bulbs? Visitors to *Made in America* can turn the cranks on this unique machine and find out for themselves.

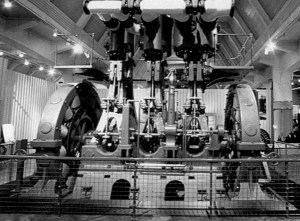

▲ "EXPLODED" MODEL T - This 1923 Ford Model T has been displayed in "exploded" form to show how many of the parts and materials came together during production. The *Made in America* exhibition illustrates how manufacturing techniques in the United States improved during the Industrial Revolution. New technology created many affordable consumer products that dramatically changed the way people lived and worked during the early twentieth century.

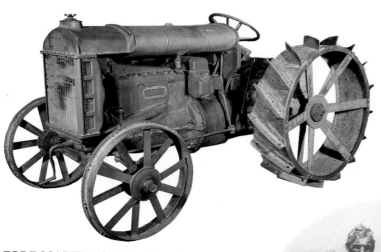

▲ FORDSON TRACTOR - Henry Ford Museum has one of America's finest collections of agricultural equipment and machinery. Henry Ford grew up on a farm but he disliked the drudgery of everyday farm chores. To help make farm work more efficient, Henry Ford and his son, Edsel *(inset photo)* developed a popular tractor in 1917. Called the "Fordson," this rugged tractor soon proved itself to be the "Model T of the soil." This is Model #1—the first Fordson tractor to roll off the assembly line.

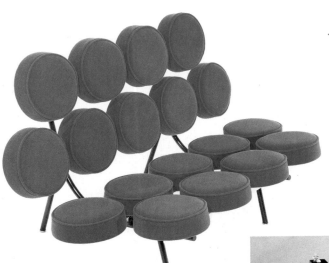

MARSHMALLOW SOFA - Named for the shape of its eighteen round seat cushions, this unusual piece was created by the Herman Miller Company of Zeeland, Michigan. The museum has a large furniture collection which illustrates how the design and construction of home furnishings have changed over the years.

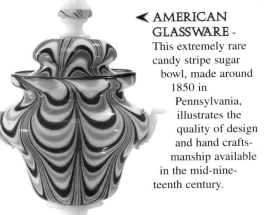

TREADLE SEWING MACHINE - Innovation and change can be seen in the most common everyday objects. The museum's collections include thousands of artifacts representing the tools and devices that were used in American homes. Foot-powered treadle sewing machines like this one, made by the White Sewing Machine Company, were very popular with women all across the country.

AMERICAN GLASSWARE - This extremely rare candy stripe sugar bowl, made around 1850 in Pennsylvania, illustrates the quality of design and hand craftsmanship available in the mid-nineteenth century.

COLUMBIAN PRINTING PRESS - The museum displays numerous communication devices from typewriters and telephones to radios and printing presses. This highly decorated example is made of cast-iron and was built around 1815 by George Clymer, the man who invented the first American iron press. The radical design did not catch on in the United States, so Clymer moved to England and made a fortune making and selling printing presses throughout the British Empire.

▲ **1930'S ~ ERA KITCHEN** - The monitor top refrigerator, Hoosier cabinet, and linoleum floor of this 1930s kitchen were once considered to be state-of-the-art advancements. A special exhibit compares this kitchen with those from the years 1790, 1840 and 1890 to illustrate how new technology and materials affected the daily lives of men, women and children.

▲ **AMERICAN CLOCKS** - Improvements in technology affected all aspects of American life. As clocks and time became more important, clockmakers designed timepieces that would better meet the needs of their customers. This double dial calendar shelf clock, built in Connecticut around 1881, combined a clock with a mechanical calendar which automatically adjusted for months with different numbers of days. This and other clocks can be seen in the museum's exhibition, *Clockwork*: *American Time and Timepieces.*

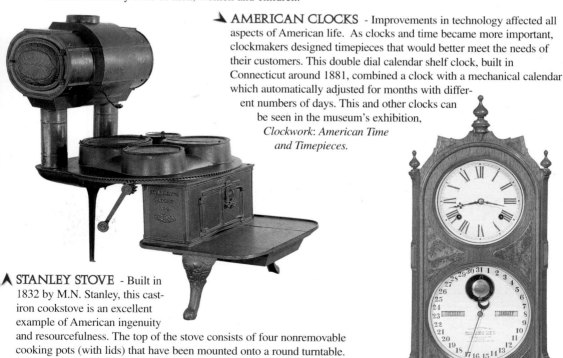

▲ **STANLEY STOVE** - Built in 1832 by M.N. Stanley, this cast-iron cookstove is an excellent example of American ingenuity and resourcefulness. The top of the stove consists of four nonremovable cooking pots (with lids) that have been mounted onto a round turntable. When the crank is turned, the entire cooking surface rotates, allowing the cook to regulate the heat in the built-in pots by moving them one by one away from the firebox. This stove even features a "no-stoop" oven to help prevent sore backs.

GREENFIELD VILLAGE

Greenfield Village never existed as a real community in the past - it was created by Henry Ford to be a giant classroom for a unique educational system of his own design. From the beginning, Ford saw the village as a site where students could follow his philosophy of "learning by doing." The artifacts and historical buildings Ford collected would help students learn firsthand about their past, and introduce them to the skills needed in a technological society.

Ford finally opened the village to the public in 1933 after public pressure to see the village mounted.

Greenfield Village consists of over 80 historic structures on an 81-acre site. Most of these buildings were brought from different parts of the United States and represent a variety of time periods. Some are the homes and workshops of famous innovators like Thomas Edison and the Wright Brothers, but the majority had less famous residents. The result is a unique history park where stories of American innovation and resourcefulness are brought to life.

The following pages include glimpses of some but not all of the historic structures that can be found in Greenfield Village.

▲ Greenfield Village

INVENTORS

Greenfield Village contains several historic structures associated with some of America's most significant innovators. In real life, though, Thomas Edison's Menlo Park Laboratory was never located as it is today, right around the corner from the Wright Brothers Home and Cycle Shop, and Henry Ford's first automobile assembly plant was not built within sight of his boyhood home. However, by bringing a number of historic structures together in Greenfield Village, Henry Ford created a special site where many national treasure buildings can be viewed and enjoyed in a single location.

◄ HENRY FORD BIRTHPLACE - Henry Ford was born and raised in this modest farmhouse, originally located about two miles northeast of Greenfield Village. Built in 1861 by Henry's father, it was home to William and Mary Ford and their six children. Henry, (the oldest child) left home at age sixteen to become a machinist in nearby Detroit.

▲ Henry Ford Birthplace was Henry Ford's first and last historic preservation project. In 1919, Ford restored the house in memory of his mother and kept the structure on its original location. In 1944, Ford decided to move the building into Greenfield Village. Henry Ford Birthplace looks as much as possible as it did in 1876 - the year Henry's mother died.

BAGLEY AVENUE SHOP -
In 1896, Henry Ford was working at a power plant in Detroit and living in a rented house on 58 Bagley Avenue. In a workshop behind the house he built his first automobile, which he called the "Quadricycle." Ford soon discovered that the vehicle was too wide to fit through the door! Henry had to widen the opening with an axe before he could take his first car out for a test drive. Ford built this replica of the Bagley Avenue Shop in Greenfield Village using bricks from the original site.

◀ Henry Ford driving the Quadricycle, October 1896.

▲ ANTIQUE AUTOS - Henry Ford started the Ford Motor Company in 1903 in Detroit. By 1913, he had perfected the moving assembly line which made automobiles affordable for just about everyone. Visitors can see, hear and occasionally ride in a variety of vintage automobiles in Greenfield Village. Shown here is a 1929 Ford Model A station wagon. In the background is a one-quarter-scale replica of the Mack Avenue Plant, the building in Detroit where Ford cars were first assembled between 1903-1905.

MENLO PARK

Menlo Park was Thomas Edison's "invention factory." From 1876 to 1882, Edison and his skilled assistants created an amazing assortment of products, including the phonograph, the electric light bulb (plus all the wires, generators, dynamos, etc. needed to create an electrical lighting system), and the mimeograph machine. Edison also made significant improvements to the telephone, telegraph and electric railway. Perhaps Edison's greatest invention was the laboratory itself: Menlo Park was the world's first industrial research laboratory.

▲ OFFICE & LIBRARY - Edison's Menlo Park laboratory complex consisted of six buildings. The brick office and library was the nerve-center of Edison's invention process. Henry Ford and his architects relied on original drawings and photographs, as well as the memories of some "old timers" in re-creating the complex in Greenfield Village almost fifty years later.

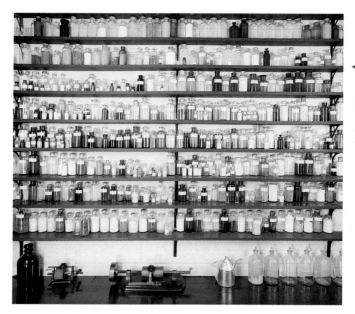

◀ 2500 BOTTLES OF CHEMICALS - Edison kept his laboratory supplied with the finest scientific equipment then available. He also kept a wide selection of chemicals and other materials on hand in the event they were needed for any unanticipated research project.

▲ The second floor of the main laboratory building was where many of Edison's most famous inventions were created. During dedication ceremonies for Greenfield Village on October 21, 1929 - the fiftieth anniversary of the invention of the light bulb - Edison sat in the wooden armchair shown at the center of this photo. After Edison left the building, Henry Ford had a workman nail the chair to the floor.

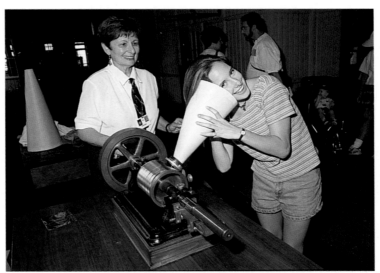

▲ A visitor listens to her voice being played back on a replica of one of Thomas Edison's early phonographs in the main laboratory building. To make a recording, a person has to shout loudly into the paper cone while the phonograph's crank is turned. Sound waves cause a needle to cut grooves onto a thin sheet of tin foil. When the process is reversed, faint sounds can be heard when the recording is played back.

Many of Edison's unmarried employees rented rooms at the Sarah Jordan Boardinghouse, located just down the street from the Menlo Park Laboratory Complex. Up to sixteen boarders could be accommodated in the six upstairs bedrooms. Mrs. Jordan, her daughter, and a maid lived on the main floor.

In 1879, Sarah Jordan's Boardinghouse became one of the first buildings in the world to be lighted by Edison's new electrical system. But since the light bulbs (mounted on the wall in this room) were experimental, Mrs. Jordan and her boarders relied on kerosene lamps as well.

Henry Ford and Thomas Edison remained close friends all their adult lives. In this photo, taken in 1930 at the dedication of the Menlo Park Glassblowing House, Edison *(right)* holds a replica of his 1879 light bulb while Ford *(left)* holds a modern light bulb from 1930.

THE WRIGHT BROTHERS HOME AND CYCLE SHOP

The Wright Brothers were self-taught engineers who used the skills they learned repairing and building bicycles to design, build and fly man's first successful airplane. This two-story frame house, originally from Dayton, Ohio, was home for the family of Milton and Susan Wright, and it is where Orville and Wilbur grew up. The two brothers also operated a bicycle rental and repair business in the Wright Brothers Cycle Shop. It was here that the Wright Brothers constructed the airplane they would use to make man's first controlled flight in a powered aircraft.

Henry Ford acquired the buildings in 1937, and with Orville Wright's assistance, restored them both to their appearance in 1903 – the year the Wright Brothers made their historic flight.

▲ WRIGHT BROTHERS HOME - Originally located at 7 Hawthorne Street in Dayton, Ohio, this house was equipped with gas lighting, a multi-burner gas range, and a water pump in the kitchen.

➤ Wilbur *(left)* and Orville Wright sitting on the porch of their family home in Dayton in 1910. Orville was born in this house in 1871; Wilbur died here after a bout with typhoid fever in 1912.

▲ Orville and Wilbur sold, rented, and repaired bicycles at the Wright Brothers Cycle Shop, originally located at 1127 West Third Street in Dayton, Ohio.

➤ The Wright Brothers built all of the components of their first gliders and airplanes in this workshop located at the back of the Cycle Shop. The original tools are still in place, next to a partial replica of the wooden center section of Orville and Wilbur's 1903 Flyer.

◄ Orville and Wilbur Wright solved engineering problems by debating issues with each other. Visitors to Greenfield Village frequently encounter actors portraying the Wright Brothers and can listen in on their spirited discussions.

AGRICULTURE

Greenfield Village offers visitors the opportunity to experience what life on the farm was like during several different periods of American history. From pre-industrial farmsteads where tools and equipment were hand-made, to more modern farms where mass-produced goods and mechanization were widely available, the agricultural sites in Greenfield Village demonstrate how farming and farm life was practiced in the eighteenth, nineteenth, and early twentieth centuries.

▲ DAGGETT FARM - Samuel Daggett, a housewright by trade, built this house around 1750 near what is now Andover, Connecticut. His house, which was moved to Greenfield Village in 1977, offers visitors a glimpse of rural life in America before the Revolutionary War.

▲ Daggett Farm depends on its large garden, to provide food that is dried and preserved for use during the winter months, as well as herbs and other plants that will be used to create natural dyes to color wool yarn.

▲ Before the advent of iron stoves, families cooked over large kitchen fireplaces, like the one in Daggett Farmhouse. Today, presenters in clothing of the period prepare daily meals using the fireplace. In addition, the presenters card and spin wool, then weave cloth on a loom.

GEORGE WASHINGTON CARVER MEMORIAL - Henry Ford had this cabin built in 1943 as a tribute to the African-American agricultural scientist, George Washington Carver. The exterior of the building was designed to be a replica of the Missouri slave cabin where Carver was born. The interior houses a small bedroom where Carver once slept, as well as an exhibit about Carver's achievements.

George Washington Carver *(left)* and Henry Ford sampling some "weed salad" (made of dandelion leaves and other greens), in 1943. Ford shared Carver's interest in new crops like peanuts and soybeans. Ford introduced soybeans to Michigan farmers and his chemists created a variety of soybean-based products including horn buttons and gearshift knobs for cars, plastics, paints, food substitutes - even a soybean suit which Henry Ford wore on occasion.

Carver spent forty years teaching southern farmers the value of new crops like peanuts and soybeans. Today, this teaching continues as actors portraying George Washington Carver demonstrate how to make peanut butter from scratch.

FIRESTONE FARM - On this 1880s living historical farm, presenters in period clothing re-create daily activities of an eastern Ohio farm family. The Firestones raised sheep, with wool being their "cash crop," but they also harvested wheat, oats, hay and corn. Harvey Firestone, who later became famous in the tire business, was born in this house. As an adult, Harvey converted the farmstead into an experimental farm. In 1984, the Firestone Family donated the farmhouse and barn to Henry Ford Museum & Greenfield Village. The buildings were moved brick by brick and board by board from Ohio and reassembled in Greenfield Village in 1985.

⌃ All of the farm work at Firestone Farm is done using horses and horse-drawn machinery. Visitors experience typical nineteenth century farm activities that change with the seasons.

➤ Firestone Farmhouse has been restored to look as it did in 1882, when Harvey Firestone's parents remodeled the house to give it a more modern appearance. The wallpaper and furnishings in the parlor, reserved for company and special occasions, show what was considered stylish during the Victorian era.

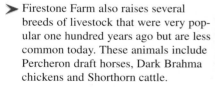 The kitchen is the center of activity year-round. Meals are prepared each day on a coal-burning stove. The recipes, clothing, furnishings and kerosene lamps are all typical of farm life in the American Midwest during the 1880s.

Wrinkly Merino sheep are raised at Firestone Farm. These sheep are a unique American breed that is still a source for some of the world's finest wool. Wrinkly sheep can produce nearly twice as much wool as a smooth-skinned sheep of similar size, but the wrinkles were bred out of the animals over time because they were so hard to shear. Border collies are often used to help move the sheep from field to field.

Firestone Farm also raises several breeds of livestock that were very popular one hundred years ago but are less common today. These animals include Percheron draft horses, Dark Brahma chickens and Shorthorn cattle.

THE VILLAGE GREEN

Greenfield Village has been laid out in the manner of a small New England community with a large open field, called the Village Green, at its center. Surrounding the Green are a number of public buildings including a chapel, an inn, a courthouse, a general store, and a town hall. Today, the Village Green is where a host of programs and special weekend activities take place.

⋏ LOGAN COUNTY COURTHOUSE - This building, originally from Postville (now Lincoln), Illinois, served as the seat of county government and for community gatherings in the 1840s. Henry Ford brought the courthouse to Greenfield Village in 1929.

⋏ During the 1840s, lawyers traveled the circuit from one county courthouse to another, holding court in rural communities like Postville twice a year. During these occasions the residents of the area packed into town to purchase supplies and catch up on the latest gossip. They also crowded around the courthouse, listening to the proceedings through open windows.

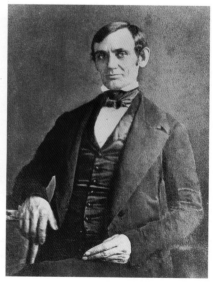

⋏ One of the circuit-riding lawyers who tried cases in the Logan County Courthouse was Abraham Lincoln, shown here as he looked around 1850.

MARTHA-MARY CHAPEL - Henry
Ford built six non-denominational chapels
around the United States in honor of his
mother, Mary Litigot Ford, and his moth-
er-in-law, Martha Bryant. This chapel was
built in Greenfield Village in 1929.
In front of the chapel stands the "Garden
of the Leavened Heart." This unusual garden, filled with a mixture of culinary
herbs, ornamental herbs and flowering
ornamental plants, was originally developed in 1938 by Clara Bryant Ford,
Henry Ford's wife.

CLARA BRYANT FORD
1867-1950
This portrait was made
around 1918.

Although no regularly scheduled services are held,
the chapel is used for wedding ceremonies and other
special programs throughout the year.

◄ EAGLE TAVERN - Built in 1831 about fifty miles west of Detroit in Clinton, Michigan, the Eagle Tavern was originally a stagecoach stop for travelers on the Detroit-to-Chicago road.

➤ Today visitors encounter the Eagle Tavern as it appeared in the 1850s when Calvin Wood owned the tavern. All items on the menu have been adapted from 1850s recipes and travelers today may find themselves talking about 1850s politics with an actor portraying Calvin Wood or a member of his family.

◄ GAMES ON THE GREEN - During warm weather, Greenfield Village offers children of all ages the opportunity to participate in a variety of old-fashioned American games like spinning tops, walking on stilts, and rolling hoops.

◄ J.R. JONES GENERAL STORE &
THE LAH-DE-DAHS - Built in
Waterford, Michigan in 1854, this
building operated as a grocery store
and post office until 1927 when it was
brought to Greenfield Village. In the
1880s, J.R. Jones, the store proprietor,
helped sponsor a baseball team called
the Lah-de-Dahs. During the summer,
visitors are often invited to play spirited games of "town ball" on the Village
Green, or to watch the modern-day
Lah-de-Dahs in action.

▲ The general store has been restored to look as it did in the 1880s, when Waterford
was a resort community that drew in large numbers of vacationers from cities like
Detroit and Lansing during the summer months. The general store carried a wide
variety of goods for its customers, as well as the town's only telephone!

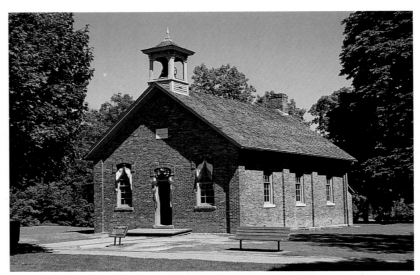

➤ SCOTCH SETTLEMENT SCHOOL - Seven-year-old Henry Ford started school in this one-room schoolhouse, originally in Dearborn, Michigan, in 1871.

⋀ In the nineteenth century, American children received a basic education in geography, writing, reading, mathematics and American history, as well as lessons in Christian morals and the virtues of hard work. Students from first through eighth grades learned together in a one-room classroom, all taught by the same teacher.

➤ Teachers of one-room schoolhouses rang a bell to announce that school was in session. Today visitors are invited to attend class and participate in lessons taught as they were in the 1870s.

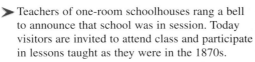

TOWN BUILDINGS

Although not patterned after any particular historic town, Greenfield Village includes many of the same types of structures that would have been found in small communities all across America in the nineteenth century. In additon to farmhouses, workshops and the buildings around the Green, the Village has such typical structures as stores, shops, mills, a railroad depot and a bandstand.

◄ COHEN MILLINERY SHOP - From 1892-1903, Mrs. Elizabeth Cohen made her living decorating women's hats in this building, originally located in Detroit. This shop was one of a new wave of urban, specialized retail stores that catered to middle-class working families.

➤ Mrs. Cohen purchased ready-made hat bodies from manufacturers, then trimmed them to the tastes of her customers with ribbons, artificial flowers, feathers and buttons. She also sold various fabrics, notions, and gentlemen's accessories (ties, cuff links and shirt collars). Today, costumed presenters continue to trim hats in the Cohen tradition.

◄ GRIMM JEWELRY SHOP - Englebert Grimm sold and repaired watches, clocks and jewelry in this shop from 1886-1931, originally located in Detroit. Henry Ford was a frequent customer and brought the building to Greenfield Village after Mr. Grimm's death. The building is restored to its appearance in the late-1880s.

▲ SIR JOHN BENNETT SHOP - Gog and Magog, two mythical English giants who guarded the city of London, tolled the Westminster Chimes each quarter hour from 1846 to 1929 above Sir John Bennett's Jewelry Shop in London, England. Henry Ford had his architect trim the original five-story building down into a smaller two-story structure that has become a village landmark.

◄ EDISON ILLUMINATING COMPANY "STATION A" - One of Thomas Edison's early power plants, Station A supplied direct current (DC) electricity to Detroit homes and businesses between 1886-1900. Coal-burning boilers drove steam engines which were connected to dynamos on the second floor. Henry Ford built this one-quarter scale partial replica in Greenfield Village in 1944.

➤ In 1893, Henry Ford (*far left*) was the chief engineer at Station A. Henry could have had a comfortable career in the electric power business, but he left it in 1899 to try a risky new venture: designing gasoline-powered automobiles.

CRAFTS & TRADES AREA

Greenfield Village is well-known for its excellent crafts programs. Visitors enjoy seeing demonstrations of glass blowing, pottery making, printing, weaving and tinsmithing. Other buildings contain a steam-powered machine shop, a silk mill, and a mechanized wool carding mill. Many of the products created in the various craft demonstration buildings can be purchased in the Museum and Village stores.

▲ Crafts & Trades Area.

▲ GLASS PLANT - In the Glass Plant, skilled craftspersons demonstrate traditional glass production techniques, such as "free-blown glass," in which a glassblower gathers molten glass on the end of a blow pipe and shapes it with various tools.

▲ POTTERY SHOP - In the Pottery Shop, visitors see the complete process of making pottery, from mixing and forming the clay to decorating, glazing and firing it in the kiln.

◄ TEXTILES
DEMONSTRATION -
Skilled weavers operate the
colonial fly shuttle loom. An
experienced weaver can weave
about twelve inches of fabric
an hour on a loom like this.

➤ PLYMOUTH CARDING MILL -
As a boy, Henry Ford frequently
accompanied his father on trips to
take wool to this carding mill, originally located in Plymouth, Michigan.
Mechanical carding machines, like
the one shown here (made around
1850), used a series of rollers cov-
ered with metal brushes to comb,
straighten and roll the wool into
long, fluffy "rovings."

◄ PRINTING
DEMONSTRATION - This build-
ing specializes in "job printing" - the
printing of small, special order items
like business cards and flyers. A variety of presses are demonstrated, from
powered platen presses, to early
American printing presses, like the
Washington Press shown here.

ARMINGTON & SIMS MACHINE SHOP - Built in Greenfield Village in 1929, this building replicates a job shop from the early 1900s. The machine shop was the site of much innovative problem-solving that drove the Industrial Revolution.

A young "machinist" learns firsthand what is involved in making a miniature candlestick out of a brass rod, using the 1917 Brown & Sharp turret lathe.

TINSMITH SHOP - Tin-plate was the nineteenth century equivalent of plastic: a lightweight, cheap, attractive material for pots, pans, lamps and hundreds of other utensils. Tin, often called the "poor man's silver" was sold to the rich and poor alike by traveling tin peddlers. Today, craftspeople make a selection of tinware, all based on historic artifacts in the museum's collections.

A visitor tries her hand at making a pierced tin keepsake.

─HISTORIC HOMES─

A number of historic homes can be found along the tree-lined streets of Greenfield Village. Some, like the Noah Webster House, are imposing structures associated with a famous person. However, the majority are modest dwellings that were occupied by average, lesser-known individuals. The homes located throughout the Village represent a variety of architectural styles, time periods and social classes.

◄ NOAH WEBSTER HOUSE - Noah Webster was sixty-five years old in 1823 when he moved into this house, originally in New Haven, Connecticut. During his long life, Webster had been friends with George Washington, learned twenty languages, lectured nationwide, and written a basic reader (nicknamed "The Blue-Backed Speller") that became the most popular book in America, second only to the Bible.

► Webster completed his dictionary, which included 70,000 handwritten entries, in this second-floor study. Webster had over 1000 books in his personal library when he died in 1843. The total value of these volumes at that time well exceeded the value of all the furnishings in the house.

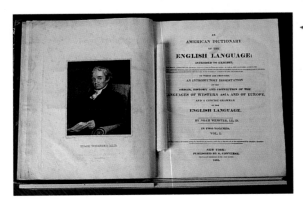

◄ In 1825, Webster completed his masterwork, *The American Dictionary of the English Language*, after spending twenty-five years researching the book. He saw the book through two printings before his death.

COTSWOLD COTTAGE - Originally built in England around 1620, Cotswold Cottage was purchased by Henry Ford in 1929. The house, barn and fences – all made of native limestone – were taken apart stone by stone and sent by ship to the United States. Today Cotswold Cottage, surrounded by a Victorian flower garden, is one of the most picturesque buildings in the village.

COTSWOLD FORGE - Built in the early 1600s, this forge has been operated almost without interruption for 300 years!

CAPE COD WINDMILL - Hundreds of windmills like this one dotted the east coast of America during the 1600's. These windmills used strong ocean breezes to provide power for grinding grain into flour. This windmill was moved to Greenfield Village in 1936. In the foreground, a presenter dressed in clothing typical of the 1760s, demonstrates the drop spindle, which enabled wool to be spun into yarn without a spinning wheel.

Greenfield Village blacksmiths, like the craftsmen who worked in the Cotswold Forge before them, make cooking implements, lighting devices and building materials (like nails and hinges). They heat iron in the forge and shape it with hammers against an anvil.

AFRICAN-AMERICAN
FAMILY LIFE & CULTURE

Many of the buildings in Greenfield Village illustrate how resourceful and innovative people can be, even in the face of extreme hardship. The African–American sites in Greenfield Village explore the various opportunities and restrictions faced by both enslaved workers during the 1860s and free black farmers in the 1930s.

▲ MATTOX HOUSE - Originally built in the 1880s, this house was the home of several generations of the Mattoxes, an African-American family who owned and worked a farmstead near Savannah, Georgia.

▲ The Mattox House has been restored to its appearance in the 1930s. During this period when money was scarce, southern families frequently papered their walls with newspapers and pages from mail order catalogs. This innovative decoration was an inexpensive form of wallpaper and also helped insulate the house against cold winds.

▲ Food writer and chef Howard Paige demonstrates authentic African-American recipes during a special event weekend at the Mattox House.

➤ HERMITAGE SLAVE HOUSES - These two small buildings came from the Hermitage Plantation near Savannah, Georgia, which was famous throughout the South for the superior bricks it produced. The Hermitage was an industrial plantation which relied on highly skilled enslaved workers. Plantation owner Henry McAlpin originally had fifty-two of these brick houses, arranged in a rectangle formation, to house the 200 enslaved workers who operated the 288-acre plantation.

◀ The interior of this house may look comfortable to a modern visitor, but the people who once lived here were enslaved and could not determine their own destinies.

▲ SUSQUEHANNA PLANTATION - In contrast to the Hermitage Plantation, the Susquehanna Plantation was an agricultural operation whose enslaved workers were basically unskilled and lived in wooden shacks with dirt floors. The design of the main house, with its long, wide porches on either side, was very common in the Tidewater Region of Maryland. Planter Henry Carroll lived with his wife and children in this home during the 1860s. The building originally sat on a 700-acre plantation operated by seventy-five enslaved workers.

▲ Actors at the various plantation sites in Greenfield Village periodically present dramatic plays that explore the impact of slavery on both the enslaved worker and the slave owner's family.

TRANSPORTATION

Many historic modes of transportation are demonstrated in Greenfield Village. Visitors have the opportunity to ride on a train pulled by a steam locomotive, sail on a paddle wheel steamboat, tool around the village in an antique bus, or receive a narrated tour in a horse-drawn carriage. In addition, they can talk with the engineers, firemen, drivers and mechanics who operate this historic machinery and keep it in good running order.

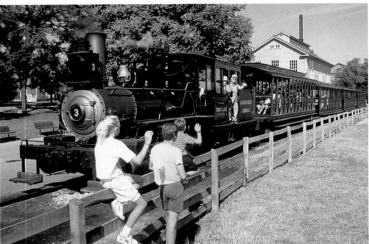

RAILROAD - Several steam-powered locomotives are operated in Greenfield Village, including the *Torch Lake*. Built in 1873, it is the oldest continuously running locomotive in the United States. From April 1 to mid-October, visitors can ride completely around the Village, getting on and off at three different stations.

SMITHS CREEK DEPOT - As a boy, Thomas Edison worked out of this depot, selling newspapers to passengers traveling by train between Detroit and Port Huron, Michigan. The depot was built around 1859. Today, the depot is active again. Amtrak has developed a special schedule allowing train travelers to disembark directly into Greenfield Village.

RAILROAD TURNTABLE - Visitors demonstrate that the 25-ton *Edison* locomotive can be turned with ease using this hand-operated turntable.

ANTIQUE BUS - This 1931 Ford Model AA bus shuttles visitors from the far end of the village back to the main entrance.

CAROUSEL - Built in 1913, this Herschell-Spillman Carousel was moved to Greenfield Village from Liberty Lake, Washington. It features a variety of exquisitely carved wooden animals. Visitors can ride the carousel from April 1 to mid-October.

STEAMBOAT - The steamboat *Suwanee* is named after a paddle steamer Thomas Edison rode during his winters in Florida. This vessel was rebuilt in 1988 and uses the same engines Henry Ford salvaged from the original *Suwanee* in 1930. Passengers can sail around the Suwannee Lagoon on the steamboat from Memorial Day to Labor Day.

HORSE-DRAWN CARRIAGE - A narrated carriage ride is one of the more popular ways of seeing Greenfield Village at a leisurely pace.

SPECIAL EVENT WEEKENDS

Henry Ford Museum & Greenfield Village sponsors a number of Special Event Weekends each year. Each event features special programming and offers visitors the opportunity to participate in a number of interactive hands-on activities. Below are examples of just some of the Special Events Weekends that take place in Greenfield Village during the year.

▼ MOTOR MUSTER

▲ SPRING FARM DAYS

>
CIVIL WAR
REMEMBRANCE

▼ SALUTE TO AMERICA CONCERTS

➤ OLD CAR FESTIVAL

▲ FALL HARVEST FESTIVAL

▲ RAILROAD DAYS

▲ TRADITIONS OF THE SEASON

HENRY FORD ACADEMY
OF MANUFACTURING ARTS & SCIENCES

In 1929, Henry Ford established the Greenfield Village Schools, a unique school system that operated in the one-room school houses and other buildings in the village. Ford believed in the philosophy of "learning by doing" and he hoped to inspire students by immersing them in the environment of the past so that they could better prepare for success in the future. This school system continued to operate until 1969.

On August 12, 1997, Ford Motor Company and Henry Ford Museum & Greenfield Village returned to their formal educational roots by establishing the Henry Ford Academy of Manufacturing Arts & Sciences. This innovative public high school academy with 100 students in each grade is chartered by the Wayne County (Michigan) Regional Educational Service Agency.

The four-year program emphasizes applying mathematics, sciences, humanities and communication skills to real-world problems. The goal is to develop and graduate young people who are ready for anything – college, skilled trade apprenticeships or jobs in a global, technological workplace.

The academy will serve as a national model for education reform and educator development by demonstrating new teaching and learning strategies as well as new ways for educators to collaborate with industry, labor, cultural organizations, higher education and other community members.

The students at Henry Ford Academy, like those who went to Henry Ford's Greenfield Village Schools between 1929-1969, are pioneers—attending high school in a new way, with new challenges and opportunities as the students, the museum, and Ford Motor Company prepare for success in a rapidly changing world.

Students learn in unique settings ranging from the exhibitions and displays inside Henry Ford Museum, to historic structures like Thomas Edison's Menlo Park Laboratory, to Ford Motor Company's high-tech facilities. The World Wide Web and other telecommunications tools link students to resources around the globe.

OTHER FACILITIES

In addition to the educational programming that visitors and student groups experience, Henry Ford Museum & Greenfield Village is utilized for a number of other purposes, including after-hours catered events, weddings, conferences and corporate training. The Museum's Education Building also houses the Research Center, an archives and research library with over 25 million documents, photos, and graphic materials.

▲ LOVETT HALL BALLROOM - Henry Ford built this ballroom with a special sprung floor for dancing. The hall is available for banquets, conferences and wedding receptions.

▲ THE RESEARCH CENTER - The museum's archival collections include automotive history, prints and photographs, the museum's institutional archives, general books and periodicals, special collections, and the Edsel B. Ford Design History Program. These materials are available for research by the general public.

▲ CATERED EVENTS can be arranged to take place after-hours on the Museum floor.

▲ WEDDINGS are scheduled year-round in a variety of museum locations, including the Martha-Mary Chapel and Memorial Rose Garden, shown here.

47

▲ Henry Ford Birthplace

"This is the only reason Greenfield Village exists - to give us a sense of unity with our people through the generations, and to convey the inspiration of American genius to our youth. As a nation we have not depended so much on rare or occasional genius as on the general resourcefulness of our people. That is our true genius, and I am hoping that Greenfield Village will serve that."

-Henry Ford